YASIN of Arabia

Text adapted by Nizar Jwaideh • Illustrations by Arnie Kohn

ENCYCLOPAEDIA BRITANNICA PRESS

CHICAGO   NEW YORK   LONDON

The true-to-life photographs in this book are related to the educational motion picture "Arabian Children," produced by Donald G. Hoffman, and the educational filmstrip "Family of Jordan," both issued by Encyclopaedia Britannica Films, Inc. The photographs were taken by Frank Richter in Jordan.

Nizar Jwaideh, who adapted the text of the book, was born and educated in Iraq and worked as a journalist in the Middle East for some years. He is now on the editorial staff of the Chicago "Sun-Times."

The design of this book is by Alex D'Amato. Supervision of color reproduction is by James Lockhart. The cover design is by Don Walkoe.

The book has been carefully manufactured for long wear. The paper is 100-pound coated stock specially created for this series. The pages are side-sewn and are fixed into the case with sturdy end sheets. The laminated cover resists dirt and is washable.

The body type of this book is 16-point Caledonia.

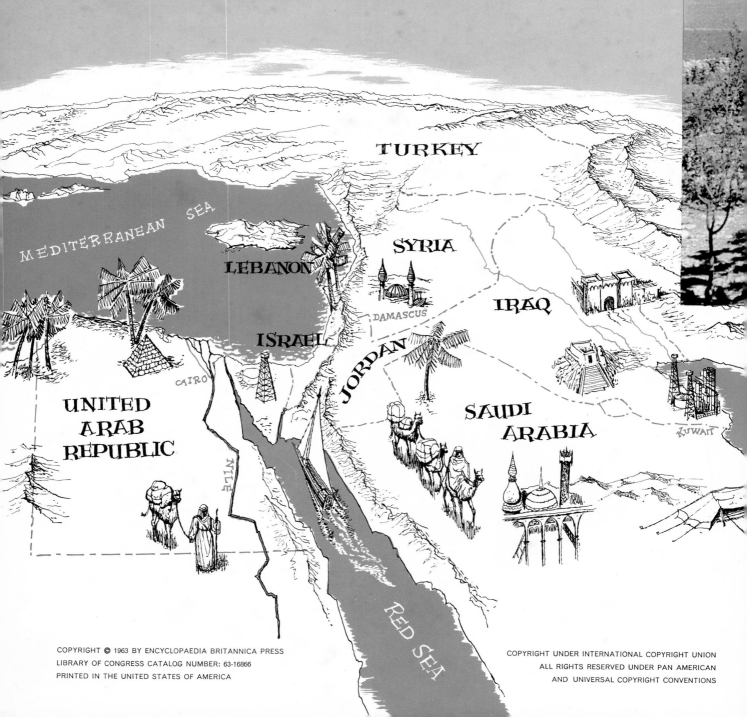

The stone houses of Saahab stand on a hill on the edge of the desert.

On the edge of the Arabian desert in the land of Jordan lies the village of Saahab. Its houses are built on a hill away from the drifting sand. The land is bare and brown, and only a few trees, bushes and patches of grass grow under the hot sun.

Most of the people of Saahab are farmers, who live on what little they can grow in the fields.

asin awoke one spring morning to the far-off jingle of many camel bells. That sound meant only one thing—the bedouins were coming to Saahab. Yasin called to his father, Ahmad, and his younger brother, Taisir, and said, "Let us go and see the bedouins."

But Ahmad said, "The bedouins do not like strangers. We can see them from our roof."

Ahmad and his sons put on their *kaffiyahs*, the cloths that protected their heads from the hot sun, and

Yasin pointed toward the bedouins as he stood on the roof with Ahmad and Taisir.

Aisha and her mother, Laila, wore long garments embroidered
with many colors, and they covered their heads with scarves.

went onto the roof. The roof was flat and the family slept here in the summer when it was too warm to sleep indoors. Yasin pointed excitedly to a long line of camels and horses, which was approaching the village from the desert.

Yasin's sister, Aisha, had arisen earlier and was downstairs helping her mother, Laila. They prepared breakfast before the boys went to school and Ahmad to the fields. Ahmad raised food for his family and could very well use the help of his sons in the fields. But he sent them to school because he knew the value of education. Ahmad could not read or write, for there had been no school in Saahab when he was a boy.

Taisir drove the sheep and the goat through the gate into the street.

Before they went to school, the boys had jobs to do. Taisir went to the courtyard to fetch the single sheep and the goat, which the family kept for their wool and milk. Taisir had named the sheep Abiad (white) and the goat Aswad (black). The animals knew their names and came when Taisir called them. He drove them into the street and took them to the village shepherd.

The shepherd was hired by the farmers of Saahab to tend their animals because they could not spare time for this themselves. Every morning the animals were collected outside the village, and the shepherd took charge of them all day.

Taisir watched while the shepherd filled cans with water for the animals.

Before leaving the shepherd, Taisir watched him fill cans with water, which he had drawn from a well in a skin bag. There was no water in the desert grazing lands, and so the shepherd gave water to the animals before starting out. He took some water along for himself.

There was little for the animals to eat around the village. The shepherd had to drive his flock far into the ravines, where some grass and bushes grew.

After the spring rain, the arid plain would be covered for a short while with a carpet of grass and

flowers. Then the animals would fatten and their milk would become plentiful.

Yasin sat behind the camel's hump as Ahmad led old Zenboor from the courtyard.

Meanwhile, Yasin went with his father to look after the young fruit trees they were growing.

In the courtyard Zenboor, the old camel, knelt down and Ahmad strapped the *mihrath*, the heavy wooden plough, and other tools to the saddle. Zenboor's name meant "wasp" in Arabic. But the camel was tired and slow and not at all wasplike.

Yasin mounted behind the camel's hump. He held on to the saddle so that he would not fall off when

Zenboor stood up and began to move with lurching, swaying steps.

Ahmad led the camel, with Yasin riding, through the winding, unpaved streets of Saahab. On the way they passed a truck, an unusual sight in this area. Camels, horses and donkeys were used for work, travel and transport, and machines were rare. Yasin was excited to see the vehicle.

"Why don't we buy a truck?" he asked his father.

"We cannot even afford a horse," Ahmad replied, pulling at the camel's rope. Zenboor had stopped to sniff the truck, and he snorted loudly.

Yasin was pleased to see the truck, but Zenboor snorted and turned away.

The wind blew Ahmad's flowing Arab robe as he led Zenboor across the desert.

Ahmad and Yasin crossed the desert ground, which was unfit for farming because it was hard and stony. They came to their young fruit trees on the slope of a hill. Ahmad had planted them there so that the rain water would reach them as it ran down the slope.

To work the land Ahmad had a simple wooden plough. He had to lean heavily on the handle to turn the dry earth. Ploughing was hard work, and some-times stones caught in the plough and broke it.

Ahmad was concerned about a young fig tree he had planted. He had covered it with stones to protect it from the sun and sand. Yasin removed the stones and saw that the tree was wilting; it needed water badly. In dry years many plants died from lack of water.

While Yasin loosened the hard earth around the fig tree with a *menjel*, or sickle, Ahmad unloaded a can for water from the camel's back. Yasin took the can and hurried to the well.

Ahmad took a can for water from the camel's back and Yasin uncovered the young fig tree.

Yasin unlocked the lid of the family well.

The well belonging to Yasin's family was covered with an iron lid and kept locked, for water was precious in the desert. Each family owned a well or shared one with another family. Most of the wells were dug a long time ago. Some of them were more than a thousand years old and were still used.

Yasin unlocked the lid and lowered the can on the end of a rope to draw water. Then he carried the can of water back to his father. On the way he watched for gazelles, the beautiful desert deer. They sometimes invaded the fields and ate the plants and fruits the farmers worked so hard to grow. Yasin wanted a gazelle for a pet, but it was not easy to catch one. Perhaps an old hunter he knew would help him.

When Yasin reached his father, Ahmad took the can and poured water around the young fig tree. As Yasin watched, he imagined the delicious taste of the figs that would ripen on the tree when it grew.

It was nearly time for school. Yasin covered the fig tree again. The stones would hide it from the gazelles.

He watched Ahmad pour water around the little fig tree.

*Y*asin met Taisir at the edge of the village and they set off together. They could hear the school bell warning them that it would be time for morning roll-call in a few minutes. The brothers joined other boys on their way through the village. The streets of Saahab were full of people going to work.

The boys walked past houses with thick walls of stone. The windows had shutters, which could be closed to keep out the sun and to keep the rooms cool.

"Hurry, hurry!" the boys said to each other. The bell had stopped, and they did not want to be late.

Yasin loved books. They taught him many wonderful things about other parts of the world. He had never been outside Saahab, but he knew about other countries and about great cities. He liked history books best and loved to read about his ancestors, the Arabs.

A boy rang a bell to summon the pupils to class.

Yasin and Taisir walked along the village street on their way to school.

Thirteen centuries ago the Arabs conquered most of the world that was then known, and founded an empire that lasted almost a thousand years.

Besides history, the boys studied the Arabic language, English, arithmetic, science, and agriculture.

Taisir was not so interested in books as Yasin was, but he liked to draw pictures. He was saving money from doing odd jobs around the village and was going to buy some colored pencils.

It was a long way to the school, and the boys hurried across the desert.

The school building was new and was built outside the village, where there was space for a large playground. The boys hurried across the desert ground to the school.

The boys stood in lines in the school yard.

Before going into school, the boys removed their *kaffiyahs* and stood in lines in the yard. They answered the roll as their names were called, and then filed into their classrooms.

Yasin was learning English. At first he was puzzled because English is written from left to right, whereas Arabic is written from right to left. The Arabic alphabet is different from the English alphabet and looks like a form of shorthand. But the two languages share the same numerals. Long ago the Western nations adopted Arabic numerals (2, 3, 4) because they were simpler to use than Roman numerals (II, III, IV).

Aisha drew water from the well and poured it into a clay jar.

Aisha helped at home while the boys were at school. She did not go to school, for in most Arab villages schooling was only for boys.

Aisha fetched water from the well. She drew the water in a skin bag and poured it into a large jar. She lifted the jar onto her head. Although she was young and small, she carried the jar easily, for she had learned to do this at an early age. She walked gracefully, balancing the jar with one hand.

The jar was made of clay and was the same shape as jars used centuries ago in Saahab. Clay jars were better than metal cans for holding water because the water seeped through pores in the clay and evaporated on the sides of the jar, thus keeping the water cool.

Sitting on the floor, Aisha and Laila prepared food for the family.

Some of the water Aisha brought was used by her mother to make bread. Laila kneaded the dough while Aisha churned goat milk into butter in a skin bag.

Although the family ate rice, vegetables and sometimes meat, their chief food was bread. It was made of barley or wheat flour.

When the dough was ready, Laila shaped it into flat, round loaves and took them to the earthern oven in the courtyard. The loaves baked slowly over the hot embers of thorn bushes.

At meal times the family sat on the floor round a low table and ate with their fingers. In the evenings Ahmad drank coffee, which Aisha brewed for him. The coffee was strong and spiced and bitter.

Laila put the loaves in the earthen oven in the courtyard.

When their housework was done, Laila and Aisha took up their needlework. They made their own clothes, which were embroidered with bright colors.

While Aisha embroidered, Laila wove a basket from colored straw. She sometimes wove table covers, too. The weaving was intricate, and the straw had to be soaked in water before it was soft enough to use.

Aisha embroidered cloth with colored thread, while Laila made a basket of straw.

Aisha used colored threads of silk or cotton for her embroidery. She did not need a pattern book, for she knew the designs by heart. They had been handed down from one generation to the next for many hundreds of years. They were simple designs of line patterns and showed no living things, because the Moslem religion forbade the portrayal of living things. The design Aisha was embroidering was similar to Arabesque designs found in many palaces and mosques of Arab countries.

Sometimes Aisha used thread made from wool, which she prepared herself. She washed the raw wool and combed it, and spun it by hand into thread. Then she dyed the thread with the colors she needed for her embroidery.

The wool Aisha prepared came from the family sheep, Abiad. One sheep did not provide much wool, but there was usually enough to make woolen yarn for knitting. Aisha kept some to knit into scarves for her brothers to wear in the winter. Even in the desert the winters are cold.

Every month Laila went to market in the neighboring town to sell the baskets she had woven and the cloth Aisha had embroidered. This brought the family a little extra money.

At mid-day the sun was high in the sky, and Ahmad was hot and tired. He and old Zenboor had been ploughing all morning. Ahmad stopped working and performed his noon prayers. Being a Moslem, he prayed five times a day. Then he rested in the shade of a rock.

The sheep huddled together, seeking the shade of each other's bodies.

Ahmad rested in the shade of a rock and drank water from an ibriq.

Ahmad drank water from an *ibriq*, a jar he had brought with him, and ate lunch of bread and dates. While he rested, he looked at the bare field he had been ploughing. He would plant it with barley this year, because he had heard that barley would fetch a good price. When he had harvested the crop, he would sell the grain to the merchants in the town.

The sun declined, and Ahmad resumed work.

Yasin and Taisir played a game like hopscotch with some friends in the village.

On the way home from school in the afternoon, Yasin and Taisir met some friends in the village and stopped to play with them. Their friends were playing a game like hopscotch. They had traced a large rectangle on the sandy ground and had divided this into squares. Each player in turn threw a stone into one of the squares. Then, hopping on one foot all the time and without touching the lines, he had to pick up the stone and throw it into the next square. The player who hopped in and out of the squares without losing his balance or touching the lines was the winner.

Yasin soon tired of the game because he considered it one for girls and small boys. Besides, he had a coin in his pocket and the candy store was not far away.

His younger brother did not want to leave the game, but the word "candy" had a magic effect. The boys did not often have money for sweets and Taisir was not going to miss this opportunity to taste some.

The brothers hurried to the candy shop. Inside were many glass jars full of sweets of different kinds. The boys could not decide which kind to buy.

"Would you like some candy from Damascus?" the shopkeeper asked them. Damascus, Syria's largest city, was famous for its candied fruit and sweets.

"When I grow up," said Taisir as they left the shop, "I shall spend all my money on candy in Damascus."

The shopkeeper helped the boys choose some candy.

At the end of the day, Yasin went to meet his father. He helped Ahmad to load the farm tools onto the camel's back and then climbed up behind them. Ahmad led Zenboor slowly home, for they were both tired.

On their way home, they neared the camp of the bedouins, whom they had seen in the morning from their roof.

"Those roving tribes are suspicious people," Ahmad said to Yasin. "But we must pass by their tents."

Ahmad did not want to go so near the camp, but the only other way home was much longer. Yasin, however, was eager to see the bedouins.

Suddenly, two men on horseback appeared from among the tents and came galloping across the desert. Ahmad stopped and watched the horsemen. They looked fierce, and their long robes flew out behind them as they rode swiftly toward him and Yasin.

Yasin knew that the bedouin warriors were sometimes dangerous. Even Zenboor trembled as the horsemen approached.

Yasin watched two bedouin horsemen galloping toward him across the desert.

The bedouins greeted Ahmad. Yasin admired their fine horses, but Zenboor snorted at them.

The two riders reined their horses a few feet from Ahmad and Yasin. They were armed with guns and daggers, and belts of cartridges were slung across their chests. Their faces were grim with suspicion. But they spoke to Ahmad.

"*Alsalamu alaikum,* peace be unto you," one of the

bedouins said, holding in his spirited horse.

"*Wa alaikum salam,* and peace to you," answered Ahmad, in the ancient greeting of the desert people.

The bedouins asked why Ahmad and his son were passing so close to their camp. Ahmad said they lived in the village and that they were going home.

The bedouins were satisfied and shook hands solemnly with Ahmad. They explained that they had to watch out for thieves, who often stole their animals. Their tribe had come to Saahab for supplies for the summer season, when they would travel far into the desert in search of grazing for their herds.

Yasin admired the beautiful horses. He knew that bedouin horses were of famous stock and that they were valuable. He decided that one day he would have a fine horse to ride instead of a slow old camel.

"Go with God," the horsemen shouted as they galloped off toward their camp. Yasin gazed after them.

They went slowly home as the sunset glowed on the walls of the old fort.

In the village, Zenboor stopped to scratch his long neck on the rough stones of the old fort. Yasin looked up at the walls, which had been built by the Ottoman Turks centuries ago and which were pink in the light of the setting sun. It was a beautiful sunset; but Yasin was hungry.

"Come on, old camel," he said. "We cannot make a meal of these stones."